CW01665632

DYING

Jonny Zucker Illustrated by Katmo

Ginn

Chapter 1
Down into the Darkness

"Goal!" shouted Chantel Lewis.

Her younger brother, Chris, scowled at her.

"No way!" he yelled. "It missed by miles and you know it."

"It was easily in!" said Chantel.

"Forget it," he replied, and kicked the ball back to Chantel.

They were playing football in the corridor outside their flat, on the tenth floor of a large tower block. It was a Saturday afternoon in late September. The sun was shining outside but an autumn breeze cooled the air.

As usual, Chantel was trying to boss Chris around, but he wasn't having it. *She can't always get her way*, he told himself. Chantel was about to speak again, when a door flew open and the angry face of their next-door neighbour, Mr Spreen, glared at them.

"How many times do I have to tell you?" he barked menacingly. "I can't bear the sound of you two kicking that stupid ball against my wall. Go somewhere else or I'll call the police. Now scram!"

Frank Spreen was the grumpiest neighbour you could wish for. He was in his mid-sixties and his main aim in life was to live in peace and quiet. He was always moaning at Chantel and Chris about making too much noise, particularly Chris.

Chantel picked up the ball and winked at Chris. Then she pressed the lift button.

"Let's go and play downstairs," she said.

The tarmac next to the basement car park was a bit of an uneven surface for playing football, but at least down there Mr Spreen wouldn't be on their case.

"See you later, Mr Spreen," said Chris, pulling a face at him.

Mr Spreen scowled and slammed his door.

A minute later the lift arrived and Chantel and Chris got in. Chantel pressed the basement button and the lift headed downwards.

"Mr Spreen is such a pain," moaned Chris.

"He's not that bad," Chantel said.

"He's worse!" Chris snapped. "It's all right for you. It's me he always picks on."

As Chris finished his sentence, the electronic sign above the lift doors showed *B*. They stepped forward expecting the doors to open.

But nothing happened.

Chris raised his eyes to the heavens. The lift was always breaking down. Last week it had been out of action for three days. The week before that it had only worked on Tuesday. He pressed the Open Doors button. Nothing happened.

"Why don't they just put in a new lift?" tutted Chantel, drumming her fingers impatiently on the lift wall. They waited, but the doors stayed firmly closed.

"Let's go up a level," said Chris. "It might just be the basement that's having a problem." He jabbed at the ground-floor button.

"Whatever," said Chantel, flicking a strand of hair out of her face.

Suddenly, with a clanking sound, the lift started moving again.

But it didn't go up. It went down.

"What's going on?" asked Chris with surprise. "The basement's the lowest level. We can't be going down!"

"It's probably nothing," replied Chantel, looking at the electronic display. It had gone blank.

"Maybe the lift's doing some sort of safety-check on itself," Chantel suggested.

"Lifts don't do safety-checks on themselves," said Chris sharply.

The lift carried on descending slowly and then came to a halt.

"I don't like it," said Chris. "We must be well below the basement now."

"I'm sure it's fine," Chantel reassured him. "I bet in a few seconds we'll be up on the ground floor and everything will be okay."

She reached for the ground-floor button, but before she could touch it the lights suddenly went out and the lift began moving down again.

Except this time it wasn't slow.

The lift quickly picked up speed.

As Chantel and Chris yelled out in panic, the lift hurtled downwards, and the sheer force of movement threw them both onto the floor.

Chapter 2
A Strange Light

Chantel and Chris screamed as they rolled across the floor. Suddenly, the lift jolted to a standstill.

They were flung against the side of the lift, like marbles smashing against a playground wall. Chantel and Chris desperately clung to each other in terror.

The lift lights flickered back on.

Then the doors finally opened.

At first, they were frozen with fear, but then cautiously they got to their feet and peered out.

Directly facing them was a dimly lit tunnel. They could just about see that the tunnel walls were streaked with thick cobwebs. A strange orange glow was coming from the far end of the tunnel.

"Where are we?" whispered Chantel.

"Don't know," Chris replied. "But let's get out of here."

He reached for the panel of lift buttons.

"Not yet," said Chantel quietly, her eyes wide with fear and excitement. "Surely we've got to explore a bit. I mean, how often does a lift go below its lowest floor?"

"I don't know and I don't really care," hissed Chris. "Now come on, before we're trapped down here forever."

But Chantel had already stepped out of the lift and was walking down the tunnel.

Chris groaned. He hated his sister when she was like this - bossy and strong-willed. He sighed deeply and followed her.

As Chantel and Chris walked, their footsteps echoed on the grimy, black path inside the tunnel. It was cold and damp. There were cobwebs on the cobwebs. It looked like no one had been down there for years.

"What is this place?" murmured Chantel.

"And why has no one ever told us about it?" asked Chris. "We know everyone in this building, but I've never heard anyone mention it before. Have you?"

Chantel shook her head.

The tunnel was about 20 metres long and at the end it curved round to the left. Chris held back. Every bone in his body was screaming *Turn back now!* But he walked beside Chantel as they followed the path's curve.

Rounding the corner, they came upon a sight that made them stand completely still. They found themselves at the entrance of an enormous cavern. The cavern was about ten times bigger than their whole flat, with huge, black walls and a high, silver ceiling. The orange glow they'd seen was coming from candles. There were hundreds of them, all over the place. Some were on tables, others on shelves, and yet more were standing in rows on the floor. The candles were tall and thin. Each one had a strange squiggly black line down its side.

Across the cavern floor was a series of long rectangular tables, each one covered with pieces of paper of different shapes and sizes. The papers all seemed to be covered in some sort of mysterious writing.

Someone's been busy, thought Chris.

They inched forward, too afraid to speak. Eventually, Chantel nudged Chris. "None of this is in English," she said, picking up a large

piece of paper. It was covered in scribbles, notes and strange markings.

"What language is it in?" asked Chris. "What are all those dots and arrows?"

"No idea," replied Chantel. She held the paper closer to her face. It made absolutely no sense to her. Chris studied a row of candles on the ground. At that second, they both heard a strange moaning sound. It seemed to be coming from somewhere to the left of them.

Chantel put the paper down. Chris looked up. The moaning continued. Then a shuffling movement caught Chantel's eye. Pointing to a large piece of dark cloth, she nudged Chris again. "Chris, look over there."

Beneath the cloth, someone or *something* was wriggling.

The dark cloth rose into the air and then slipped to the ground. Chantel and Chris watched in horror as a hideous, twisted figure was revealed.

It had horrible, pale-yellow skin. Its eyes, mouth and nose were dark grey and seemed to be floating in its face rather than being permanently fixed in one position.

"What on earth is *that*?" mouthed Chris, gripped by the icy chill of fear.

"Haven't got a clue," whispered Chantel, "but it hasn't seen us and I'm not hanging around to wait for an introduction. Let's get out of here while we can!"

Chris nodded quickly.

They turned round as silently as they could and ran back down the tunnel and straight through the open doors into the lift.

"Let's just hope it works," said Chantel.

Chris pressed *10*. The doors closed and the lift started moving upwards. Its journey was smooth and quick.

It was only when they stepped out of the lift on the tenth floor that they realised they were both shaking.

Chapter 3
A Dark Return

A few days later, Chantel and Chris were in the lift again.

"I told you to leave it alone!" Chris said angrily. Chantel was driving him mad. She was standing inside the stationary lift, studying its panel of buttons for the millionth time.

"I don't know why you're bothering," complained Chris.

To his utter horror, since their trip to the cavern, Chantel had been desperately trying to get them back down there again. *Is she completely out of her mind?* he asked himself. She'd pushed the lift buttons over and over again. She'd flicked them in several different ways. But the basement was as far down as they ever got. And that was just fine by him.

They'd talked about whether or not to tell their mum about the creature and the cavern, but decided against it. She'd probably just say they'd been playing too many computer games and were imagining things. Adults often said things like that.

"We had a look down there," continued Chris, "just like you said we should. I went along with it. We saw the cavern, we saw that *thing*. We didn't like what we saw and we ran away. End of story."

"It's not that simple," protested Chantel. "There's something really amazing going on down there. What are all of those candles for? What's the strange writing on all of those papers? What is the creature living down there? Perhaps it's friendly."

"Yeah, like a hungry shark is friendly to an out-of-depth swimmer," snorted Chris.

"Come on," said Chantel, trying once more to look behind the panel of lift buttons. "Doesn't even a tiny part of you want to know what's going on down there?"

"No," replied Chris. "One trip below the basement was enough for me."

Chantel was about to carry on arguing, when the angry figure of Mr Spreen loomed over them.

"Not you two again!" he shouted. "You'll be the death of me! Can't you ever be quiet? If you're not kicking a football around, you're yelling and screaming. How many times do I have to tell you? Keep the noise down!"

"Sorry, Mr Spreen," said Chantel, walking away. Chris followed her.

Mr Spreen shouted after them, "You're not sorry. If you were really sorry, you'd stop annoying me. Now clear off – both of you!"

Chris cursed under his breath. "Sometimes I wish Mr Spreen would just disappear," he hissed.

The next day, after school, Chantel and Chris joined some other kids playing football on the tarmac next to the basement. When the game finished, they walked to the basement entry and pressed for the lift. As soon as it came they stepped inside, and Chantel started pushing the buttons in different orders.

"Can't you just leave it alone?" moaned Chris. "It was a freak accident. We weren't meant to go down there. Just forget it."

"Maybe you're right," nodded Chantel eventually. "Perhaps it is best left alone." She gave the panel a thump in frustration. The doors closed immediately and the lift was plunged into darkness.

"You idiot!" yelled Chris as the lift started moving downwards, picking up speed by the second.

Chantel and Chris clung tightly to the rail around the sides of the lift. Neither of them was prepared to be smashed onto the lift floor again. The lift thundered down and stopped as abruptly as before. The light came on and the doors opened.

"I can't believe we're here again," said Chris furiously. "I told you not to mess with those lift buttons."

"Okay, okay," whispered Chantel, "but now we're down here, we might as well try to find out what's happening."

"I don't want to know what's happening. I want to go – now!"

"Let's just give it one more chance," pleaded Chantel. "We'll have a quick look around and then go straight home. Promise."

Chris chewed his bottom lip for a few seconds. He reluctantly nodded.

Outside the lift everything was exactly the same as the first time: the tunnel, the cobwebs, the entrance to the cavern, the candles.

They stopped outside the cavern entrance.

There was no sign of the strange figure anywhere.

"Come on," Chantel said quietly. "The creature's not here and I want to look at those pieces of paper again. We might find something that explains what this place is all about."

They tiptoed forward and approached one of the tables. Chantel picked up a huge piece of paper and turned it round in her hands several times. Chris grabbed a smaller scrap and studied the marks on it.

"Can you understand any of it, Chantel?" asked Chris.

Chantel shook her head. "What about you?" she asked.

"Nothing," Chris replied.

"Found something interesting?" asked a deep, growling voice, from somewhere above their heads.

Chapter 4
Face of Fear

Chantel dropped her piece of paper. Chris slunk backwards into the shadows.

Looking up, they saw the same hideous figure climbing down a rope ladder, suspended from the ceiling. It was wrapped in the same brown material as before and had reached the ground. It moved menacingly towards them.

Chantel and Chris were about to turn and run, but the creature spoke again.

"Please don't go," it said quickly. "When I summoned you the first time, you fled before I had a chance to speak to you."

The creature leaned towards them and whispered. "I'm sure you'll be willing to stay longer this time."

Chantel and Chris stood rooted to the spot. The creature was definitely some sort of disfigured man, but he didn't look like anyone they'd ever seen. Up close, he looked even more horrific than before. He was like someone who'd had life completely sucked out of him. His floating facial features seemed at risk of sliding completely off his face.

"Don't be frightened, Chantel and Chris," the creature said softly. "I know I'm repulsive to look at, but I mean you no harm."

The children stared at him with disbelief.

"How do you know our names?" gasped Chris.

"I know plenty about you," he said. "I know which flat you live in. I know what you had for breakfast this morning. I know you're both keen footballers. It's all recorded down here."

He waved his hand around the room, indicating the pieces of paper on the tables.

"You mean, all that stuff on the papers is about us?" asked Chris.

The creature threw back his head and laughed. It was a horrible, cackling laugh that seemed to go on forever. Then he spoke again, his voice switching to a quiet, sinister tone. "Your notes only take up a little space. If I only stored information about you two, then this place would be almost empty. No, my research stretches far further than Chantel and Chris Lewis. I know things about everyone in this block."

Chantel and Chris looked round the cavern nervously.

"What else do you know about us then?" asked Chris.

The creature sighed.

"I know what was in your school reports. I know what food you like to eat. I know who your friends are. I know all about your games in the corridor and the mean-hearted, interfering idiot called Mr Spreen. You allow him to get away with too much. Someone needs to teach him a lesson."

"He's only a grumpy old man," said Chantel quickly, suddenly feeling defensive about their grouchy neighbour.

"What's Mr Spreen got to do with you and this place?" asked Chris. "Who are you? And how do you know so much about us?"

The creature raised a hand to his face and scratched one of his eyebrows. He seemed to be lost in thought.

"Can I trust you?" he eventually asked.

Chantel glanced at Chris. They both shrugged their shoulders.

"It depends on what you tell us," said Chris.

"I'm prepared to tell you everything about myself and my work down here," said the creature. "But in return, I'm trusting you not to tell any adults about me or this place. You may tell as many children as you like, but once adults get to hear of me, they will start interfering in their nosy way. Do you understand me?"

Chantel and Chris nodded fearfully.

The creature pulled at several white cloths and revealed a circular, wooden table and three tall, wooden chairs. He sat down on one of the chairs and indicated to Chantel and Chris to sit opposite him.

"I suppose it's okay to talk to you for a bit," said Chantel, sitting down.

Chris remained standing.

"Sit, young man," said the creature. "There's nothing to be frightened of."

Chris waited a few more seconds, then edged towards the remaining chair.

The figure studied their scared faces in the glow of the candlelight.

"My name is Yardlin," he began, staring intently at the children. "For many years my people lived with humans in peaceful co-existence. We shared the Earth with them, spoke the same language, worked together. But there came a time when humans discovered we had special powers. They didn't like this. So they launched an attack on us."

He paused for a minute as the children gazed at him.

"My face carries the scars of that battle," he continued. "A battle that saw many of my

people killed. Those of us who survived fled underground, swearing to get our revenge on the human race. We have lived underground ever since, and none of us will ever step into the open again. We have lived underground for so long that the merest ray of the sun would destroy us."

There was an uneasy silence.

"What do you mean by 'revenge'?" asked Chantel.

Yardlin stared back at her.

"We sit in judgement," he replied, "using the very powers that humans were so scared of. We, or in this case, I, judge people. The notes and symbols on all of these papers around us are records of my notes, thoughts, and observations. They form the basis of my decisions."

"What decisions?" blinked Chris.

"If I decide that someone in this block of flats is good, then I leave them alone."

He paused. "But if I decide they are bad, then I single them out ..."

Yardlin's words hung in the air for a moment, before he finished his sentence. "... for death."

Both Chantel and Chris felt shivers running along their spines.

"That is my revenge," said Yardlin quietly. "This is our special power. We have the ability to destroy. But I have no wish to destroy the entire human race. I just want to deal with the evil ones. I get my own back in this way."

"What about the candles?" whispered Chantel.

"The candles represent the very souls of people," Yardlin explained.

Chantel and Chris looked bewildered.

"I don't understand," said Chris.

Yardlin stared into the children's eyes.

"Look at the candles carefully and tell me what you see."

"There are loads of them," replied Chris, "and each one has got a funny black line down its side."

Yardlin leaned towards Chris.

"If you look more closely, you will see that

each of these lines spells someone's name."

He reached up to a shelf, picked out a candle, and handed it to the children. They saw that the spindly writing on its side spelled Eileen Jenkins.

They knew Mrs Jenkins. She lived a couple of floors below them.

"Why is Mrs Jenkins' name on a candle?" asked Chris.

Yardlin grinned and his open mouth revealed a set of grey, rotten teeth.

"It's not just Mrs Jenkins who has a candle down here," he explained, taking the candle back. "It's every single person in this whole tower block."

Chantel looked confused. "You're saying that everyone who lives here has their own candle, with their own name written on it?"

Yardlin nodded.

"Does 'every single person' include us?" Chris asked.

Yardlin grinned again and the children saw even more of his revolting teeth.

"Yes, my friends. You both have a candle down here somewhere."

"Why does everyone have a candle?" asked Chantel.

Yardlin rubbed his chin before explaining.

"Every candle represents someone's life. If I leave the candle to burn, the person whose name it bears will continue to live. But if I judge someone to be evil, then their candle is blown out and I make sure that their life is extinguished."

"That's ... that's not possible," spluttered Chantel.

"I'm afraid it is possible," said Yardlin. "Since my people fled underground, we have lived beneath every single human dwelling, from the tiniest stone cottage to the biggest skyscraper. We watch people's candles burning and it is up to us to decide when a person's life should end. I choose the exact moment to extinguish a candle."

Chantel and Chris looked at Yardlin in stunned silence.

"Hang on a minute," said Chantel after a while. "Are you trying to tell us that if you blew out Mrs Jenkins' candle now, she'd simply drop dead, on the spot?"

Yardlin shook his head. "The harsher a person is judged, the quicker they will die. People who I decide are extremely evil will die in a matter of seconds. Others, who are bad, but not at the furthest end of the spectrum, take far longer to die. It could be a matter of hours or even days. In spite of my great powers, I cannot decide how long the process of death takes. I merely decide who is to die."

"That's horrible," said Chantel. "I don't believe you!"

Anger suddenly flashed in Yardlin's eyes. "It's the truth," he growled. "My people are the life-takers. We sit and watch the candles. We record everything about everyone in great detail. And we extinguish the candles at a moment of our choosing."

Chantel stood up abruptly. "I think we need to go," she said quickly, tugging Chris's arm.

Yardlin held out a hand. "Don't go! You are the first humans I have ever brought down here. Stay longer and I can tell you more."

Chris shook his head. "We're going now and you can't change our minds."

The angry expression suddenly returned to Yardlin's face. His mouth slipped into a cold sneer of hatred.

"You do not decide!" he shrieked. "I decide!"

But Chantel and Chris had heard enough. They were already running back down the tunnel. Behind them, they could hear Yardlin's harsh voice.

"Stay!" he screamed. "Don't you dare leave!"

Chantel and Chris ran for their lives.

Chris looked round and saw Yardlin chasing them down the tunnel. He was catching up with them by the second.

"Hurry up, Chantel!" shouted Chris urgently.

"I command you to stop!" called Yardlin.

Chris could sense Yardlin's presence directly behind him.

As they neared the tunnel's end, Chantel and Chris were horrified by what awaited them. Where the lift had been, there was nothing. It had completely vanished.

"Over there!" yelled Chantel, pointing to her left. She'd spied the bottom of a spiral staircase. They ran over and frantically began to scramble up it. Chris looked down and saw Yardlin climbing too, only a couple of steps behind him.

"You must stay!" yelled Yardlin. Yardlin reached out and one of his clammy hands grasped Chris's shoulder.

"Get off!" yelled Chris, pushing the hand away and speeding up.

Chantel and Chris flew up the seemingly endless stairs and finally reached the top.

Chantel frantically yanked at the handle of

an old door that faced them. It didn't budge at first, but when Chris leapt over to help her it shot open. They could almost feel Yardlin's breath as he closed in on them, screaming, "Don't leave!"

They tumbled through the door and slammed it behind them, hearing the long and agonising scream of their pursuer.

Chapter 5
A Deadly Gift

Chantel and Chris found themselves outside, near the tarmac by the basement. They fell to the ground, breathless, hearts pounding wildly, foreheads dotted with beads of sweat.

"We lost him," panted Chantel with relief. "It's a good job he can't ever come outside."

"What happened to the door?" asked Chris.

They stared at the wall behind them. There was no sign of the door through which they'd escaped.

"No idea," shrugged Chantel.

"I did tell you to stop playing with the lift buttons," said Chris crossly.

"I know, I know," Chantel replied. "You were right. I'm sorry. I won't ever do it again."

"Promise?"

"Promise," Chantel agreed.

They sat in silence for a few seconds as

they got their breath back.

"What do you think about the things he said?" Chris asked. "You know, about blowing candles out and killing people?"

"It's complete rubbish," she replied. "I reckon he's just some weirdo who can't live with other people and chose to live underground, like a hermit. He made up all of that stuff about his people deciding who gets to live and who dies. He probably thinks he's playing out a part in some horror film."

"But what about his face?" asked Chris. "It looked so real!"

"It's bound to be some sort of mask," Chantel replied. "Anyway, we won't be going down there again, so let's forget about him."

"Shouldn't we tell someone about it?"

"If we tell anyone, they'll never believe us. I say let's leave it," said Chantel.

Chris shrugged and then nodded. "You're probably right," he said.

That night, after dinner, Chantel and Chris were sitting on their balcony, looking out at the night sky. They were about to go in and start getting ready for bed, when the noise of a siren cut through the air. They looked over and saw an ambulance speeding onto the forecourt. As soon as the vehicle crunched to a halt, two paramedics leapt out and ran into the building.

Soon, Chris and Chantel heard shouting in the corridor and they rushed out to see what was going on. A small crowd had gathered to watch the paramedics. They were frantically knocking on Mr Spreen's door.

"What's going on?" asked Chantel.

"A man called 999," one of the paramedics told her. "He was having terrible chest pains."

"Stand back!" shouted the other paramedic as he kicked the door open. Chantel and Chris followed the two paramedics into the flat. Mr Spreen was lying on the lounge floor, seemingly lifeless, his phone still in his hand.

One of the paramedics knelt down beside him, to check his breathing.

"He's unconscious, but he's alive," she said. "We need to get him to hospital."

They lifted Mr Spreen onto a stretcher and placed an oxygen mask over his face.

"What's wrong? Is he going to be okay?" asked Chris.

"Can't say yet," replied a paramedic. "We're taking him to St Hughes."

The paramedics hurried out of the flat with Mr Spreen and pressed for the lift. Chantel and Chris watched as the lift arrived, and saw Mr Spreen being carried inside on the stretcher.

Chantel and Chris ran back inside their flat and watched over the balcony as the lights of the ambulance disappeared into the night, its siren screaming.

They stood in silence, each deep in their own thoughts.

"Are you thinking what I'm thinking?" asked Chris nervously, after a few moments.

Chantel nodded. "Yardlin told us that we allow Mr Spreen to get away with too much. He said, *someone needs to teach him a lesson.*"

They looked at each other in horror.

"Are you saying that ...?" Chris was too frightened to finish his question.

Chantel nodded. "It's too much of a coincidence, isn't it? Yardlin tells us what a bad person Mr Spreen is and then says he can 'blow out' any bad person's life."

"I thought you said that candle stuff was rubbish," said Chris.

"I don't know what I think any more," Chantel murmured.

"What can we do?" asked Chris.

"There's nothing we can do at the minute," said Chantel. "I certainly don't want to go back down there and confront Yardlin. It could just be a really weird coincidence. Maybe Mr Spreen will be fine by the morning."

But as she and Chris looked at each other, neither of them seemed convinced about this.

The next morning, Chantel and Chris walked to school, deep in thought. All day, whenever they saw each other, they talked of nothing else. As they got in the lift to go home after school, they agreed it was time to tell their mum.

"Even if she doesn't believe us, we'd be mad not to say anything," Chantel said.

"Do we tell her everything?" Chris asked.

"Yes," nodded Chantel firmly, "about the lift, the tunnel, the cavern, the candles, Yardlin – the whole thing."

The lift indicated it was just going up past the ninth floor when it suddenly stopped. Chantel pressed *10* twice and then, without any warning, the lift changed direction and began to travel downwards at great speed.

Chantel and Chris screamed as the lift pounded downwards. When it finally stopped, the doors whirred open. This time, though, they weren't at the entrance to the tunnel.

They were in the middle of Yardlin's cavern. He was sitting on one of the tall wooden chairs, with his back to them. As he heard them step out of the lift, he spun round to face them.

He was holding a candle on a silver dish.

The children saw at once the black spindly writing on the side of the candle. It spelled Frank Spreen.

The candle had been blown out.

Chantel and Chris gasped together.

Yardlin stared at their horrified faces. "I did it for you!" he shrieked. "I heard Chris say he wished Mr Spreen would 'just disappear', so I took care of him. I did what you wished for, Chris. I've made him disappear. And what do you do? You repay my kindness by deciding to tell your mother about me, even though I warned you not to tell any adults."

"HOW COULD YOU?" shouted Chris. "When I said 'disappear' I only meant for him to leave me alone. Mr Spreen's annoying, but I never wanted him dead!"

Chantel shook with fear and anger. "I can't believe you've done this," she said shakily. "Mr Spreen's just some old moaner who shouts at us. What did you think you were doing?"

Yardlin's face was a mixture of rage and hate. He stood up and pointed a finger furiously at them.

"I brought you down here to give you another chance," he screamed, "but now I see how selfish and ungrateful you are! You will suffer for your ingratitude."

Yardlin stamped angrily off towards a long table covered in candles.

Chris turned to run, but Chantel held his shoulder. "We're not going anywhere," she hissed.

Yardlin returned a minute later. He had an evil gleam in his eyes and was gripping two candles.

"Chris and Chantel Lewis, I believe," he snarled, holding the candles teasingly in front of the children's eyes. They could clearly see their names on the sides.

Chris stepped back in terror. But Chantel kept her eyes firmly locked on Yardlin's as she edged her way towards the left wall of the cavern.

CHRIS LEWIS
CHANTEL LEWIS
FRANKSPREEN

"There's no escape now!" yelled Yardlin. "I thought you two could help lift my loneliness, but it turns out that you are my enemies! There is only one thing good enough for enemies, and that is DEATH!"

He cackled with hideous laughter and stooped forward towards the two candles.

Chris screamed in terror and closed his eyes.

Chapter 6
The Dying Candles

There was absolute silence for a few seconds. Chris hardly dared open his eyes. He was sure that when he did, he'd be in a hospital bed at death's door, or inside a coffin. But when he did look, he was in exactly the same spot as before. Chantel was standing next to him, gripping his shoulder.

She pointed to the ground. Yardlin lay completely still on the cavern floor. His body was lifeless.

Vardan

"I don't understand," said Chris.

Chantel held up a candle. It had Yardlin's name on it.

"I saw it and blew it out a split second before he went to blow ours out," she said.

"He must have died so quickly because he was so evil," whispered Chris.

On the floor next to Yardlin were their candles, still burning. They picked them up carefully and put them down on a shelf.

"We've got one more thing to do," said Chantel as she stepped over Yardlin's body and started searching the cavern. A couple of minutes later she found what she had been looking for.

Frank Spreen, said the spindly letters on the extinguished candle in her hand.

Chantel leant over towards a row of candles resting on a shelf. She used the flame of one to relight Mr Spreen's candle. It took a while to catch but, when it did, it burned bright and tall. Chantel made sure it was safely secured to a shelf.

"It's time to go," said Chris.

They walked to the entrance and looked round the cavern for one last time. As they reached the end of the tunnel, they saw that the lift was back in its usual place, and the doors were open. Chris pressed button *10*.

"Somehow I feel as if we won't be coming down here again," said Chantel.

Later that evening, they were kicking a football around in the corridor when the lift doors opened and a nurse came out, pushing Mr Spreen in a wheelchair.

Seeing the children, he clasped his forehead. "How am I ever going to get better?" he shouted, covering his face with his hands. "It was you who nearly drove me to my grave."

"I've heard all about you two," winked the nurse. "Come on, Frank," she added, "don't go getting over-excited. If you keep calm, you'll be out of this wheelchair soon. Remember the doctors did say you made a remarkable recovery. Unlike anything they'd ever seen before."

She pushed him towards his flat. As he headed inside, Mr Spreen turned his head towards Chantel and Chris and gave the children a quizzical stare.

Two weeks later, Mr Spreen had made a full recovery and was back to being his usual grumpy self. He'd yelled at Chris for playing music too loudly, and at both of them for skateboarding in the corridor and shouting at each other about a lost tennis ball.

On a Sunday morning a month later, Chantel and Chris stood looking at an *Out of Order* sign beside the lift door in the basement. An engineer was shining a large torch down the lift shaft and muttering. She saw Chantel and Chris approach.

"You two live here?" she asked.

They nodded.

"Tenth floor," said Chris.

"This is very strange," she muttered to herself.

"What's strange?" asked Chris.

"Look," replied the engineer, spreading an enormous piece of paper over the floor. "I was doing a routine check on the whole lift system," she explained, "so I needed to come down here too. When I had a bit of a look around, I found that the lift shaft is far deeper than this plan shows. Look down here. The shaft should stop about two metres down from this basement level, but it goes way beyond that. I can't even see the bottom of it."

She shone her torch down again and shook her head in confusion.

"How can that be?" asked Chantel.

The engineer shrugged her shoulders. She peered down into the darkness again. "Absolutely no idea. It doesn't make any sense."

"What are you going to do?" asked Chris.

"I can't leave it," she replied. "I'm going to phone the office and book it as an urgent job. We'll come back as soon as possible and lay some metal cables across there." She pointed to the gaping black hole below the base of the lift. "Then we'll be sure the lift will never be able to slip below the basement."

"Sounds like a good idea," said Chantel.

"It's got to be done," the engineer replied with a grin. "After all, you never know what you might find down there."

Neither Chantel nor Chris spoke.

The engineer shook her head as the children walked off, whispering to each other. *Kids today*, she thought to herself, *they've got no imagination*.